T0149189

A THOUSAND SCATTERED MOMENTS

COLLECTION BY
Ellen Cowne
Beegee Elder
Chad Elder
Dallas Cowne
Keith Cowne (Posthumously)

ELLEN COWNE

authorHOUSE®

AuthorHouse™
1663 Liberty Drive
Bloomington, IN 47403
www.authorhouse.com
Phone: 1 (800) 839-8640

© *2015 Ellen Cowne. All rights reserved.*

No part of this book may be reproduced, stored in a retrieval system, or transmitted by any means without the written permission of the author.

Published by AuthorHouse 10/22/2015

ISBN: 978-1-5049-5438-9 (sc)
ISBN: 978-1-5049-5439-6 (hc)
ISBN: 978-1-5049-5437-2 (e)

Library of Congress Control Number: 2015916359

Print information available on the last page.

Any people depicted in stock imagery provided by Thinkstock are models, and such images are being used for illustrative purposes only. Certain stock imagery © Thinkstock.

This book is printed on acid-free paper.

Because of the dynamic nature of the Internet, any web addresses or links contained in this book may have changed since publication and may no longer be valid. The views expressed in this work are solely those of the author and do not necessarily reflect the views of the publisher, and the publisher hereby disclaims any responsibility for them.

THE TITLE

A THOUSAND SCATTERED MOMENTS comes from <u>SOME KIND OF RIDE</u> by Brian Andreas

"I still remember the day the world took you back and there was never time to thank you for the thousand scattered moments you left behind to watch us while we slept."

THE COVER

These are houses our family a lived in and where the scattered moments were either lived or created from the imagination.

The paintings of houses on the cover were done by Melody Mix Croft. Melody was born in Jackson, Minnesota in 1958 and at the age of eleven moved to Jacksonville, Florida. She earned a B.S., M. Ed., and a post -graduate degree in education and has taught elementary school in Georgia for 30 years. Retired from the teaching profession, she now focuses on her painting and family fulltime. She lives in Athens, Georgia and shares a painting studio with her husband.

"Painting envelopes me like the threads of a cocoon. And as a cocoon provides a safe place for a caterpillar to transform, painting allows me a safe place to examine mankind and myself."

DEDICATED TO KEITH A COWNE

To Ellen, a lover, a friend, a husband
To Beegee, Chad, and Dallas, a dedicated father
To education, an artist
And in all things, Keith was a lover of life
And a Poet

CONTENTS

These poems and stories are the products of several people in various times of their lives and about various parts of their lives. We have gathered them here in this collection to share them with you the reader. Each door in the sections below invites the reader to enter the poets ' imaginings, expressions, or reflections. Come on in.

GATHERING THE HEART

FOR KEITH

Without a white horse rescue
You became my hero
Taking me from survival
To life,
A prince with no glass slipper gauge
To help make sure our fairy tale would last.

Taking one, two, and three
With love enough to create home,
And heart enough to make
Home happen for all four.

Our ever-after meant path finding
Through forests of hospitals,
Typical teenager woes,
Unsuccessful Uncle Sam days and
College costs – all worthwhile
But taking their tax.

Mid-life I wonder if I did it right.
I know I never did anything real
Right, or important
Until you were there
Beside me, behind me-
My sustainer,
My soldier
My supporter
As I played at

Mother, teacher, administrator
And wife
Acting always my anchor
And my hero.

Ellen, August 1999
   (Written for Keith at the beginning of our empty nest
   By his wife who thinks he is a hero)

FOR ELLEN

He arrived too late,
offered only more of the same, maybe worse:
just another that would soon forget her
for the job, the kids, the club;
why trade one loss for another?
He had nothing to offer anyway;
nothing to gain;
even nothing to lose- -
she was already gone.

    Keith, 1977
        (Written for Ellen before their first date)

ANGEL

My angel,
Could it be that the same gravity
that condemns mortals to Earth
has guided you from the heavens?
More realistic, I think, is the possibility
that you have reversed this mighty force
and pulled me up to you
because I swear I feel paradise in your touch,
taste it in your mouth.
The breadth of a child's imagination could never conceive,
all of Shakespeare's words could never describe
the blessings I count absent-mindedly
everyday with you.

I feel like I have stolen your presence
from a better man; stumbled blindly into Canaan.
I regard my luck a greater gift
than the intellects of ten thousand philosophers.
It is an awesome paradox that I should praise the graces
that gave you to me, yet curse them for giving me
only one lifetime to love you in return.

Dallas, 2005

MORNING (2)

Before the first cigarette
I missed the nuzzle of my nose
against the soft beneath the
stubble of your beard
prodding a hand, no bigger than mine
to draw me into the morning.

Before the smell of coffee
I wished for the massive yellow-pink
scent of Count Polaski reminiscent
of many undisturbed breakfasts
plotting a day full of trivia
and a life of grandeur.

Before I met
an image in my mirror
I saw a reflection of a room empty of you
and I felt fear of a tomorrow,
also empty of you.

Ellen, 1977

ILIUM

"This is the Ilium," she said professor-like.
Her hand stretched to a bone near her waist,
Obvious even in the dim light.
The only bulb—60 watts over my mirror—
Caught her silver ring in its shadow.
Who was I to argue: no science since the 10th grade.
"I thought it was another name for Troy."
She laughed, knowing me better than I knew Homer.
"Oh, that's a different subject."
She was through with the lecture;
The ring was by my ear,
Lost in the hair at the back of my neck.
I wondered, ships at the ready,
if it really was.

Keith, 1975

I CUT YOUR HAIR

I cut your hair.
I hoped that like Samson,
sheared hair would curb
your power over me.

I sent you to Circe.
Needing someone to sing
You away from me, I wished
You to her peninsula and away
From my island of marriage.

I warned you about Cerebus.
His three heads-
divorce, disapproval of friends and mother,
And children's expectations
Were no match for you, and
You slew him and his trio of demons.

And you, like Odysseus, took
A trip into the unknown.
A world of children, jobs and
Mainly Medusa.
But not too much for you
my love.

I took you to Hades.
You brought me back.

Ellen, 2014

PARADISE IN ROOM 114

And I could taste the champagne in your lips,
your lips in the champagne
But knew which one tasted sweeter.
Was that a whirlpool,
Or just you and I spinning into each other
again
    and
again
    and
again?
without any sense of beginning,
without any sense of end.

I fell into you slowly
and with all of my might
        I embraced you
            embracing the night.
But every night gives way to dawn.

Still, we swore to battle that down,
made a pact to fight sleep
regardless of the cost of tomorrow---
other promises to keep.

So I held you, continued to wage war---
    Hostilities against the immortality of night.

Futile, however, for sleep comes for us all;
every night gives way to dawn,
for the moon is a broke lover
trying to move on.

The night eternal remains only in paradise,
and paradise, only in dream—
I'll meet you there,
    Waiting
    in room 114.

    Dallas, 2002

A VALENTINES DAY NOT-POEM

These words don't want to be a poem.
They want to be memories.
 I make love to Memories that help me
remember the fullness of passion when
you searched with tenderness for something
in my eyes.
I wonder if you found it there.
Or if you found it anywhere in me.

But dressed in armor of silence and criticism,
I hug close those hurtful times resurrecting each.
as if the face off would make them vanish
or, if not disappear, return to me
wrapped in a warmth rather than the chill
that sits heavy in my heart like eating too much ice cream.
I replay the scene over and over in my memory - stupid -
like touching, with my tongue, a tooth that aches
just to see if the pain is still there festering –
an open sore that no one but you can heal.

But these words don't want to be a poem.
They will go where they want, phantoms
moving my fingers like chess pieces on
a board I cannot see beyond the next move.
they insist on being memories so I'm
opening only the files not dangerous to my heart.

These words lack the strength of the arms that
woke me the morning after you
kept me in your bed all night.
Arms still wrapping me in a blanket
of safety after protecting me from dreams
that would take away my children.

These words will never have the impact
on a heart of your borrowed words,
"Any time she's gone, she's gone too long"
perched on a stick in a basket of daisies
and sent to someone who needed to be missed.

They will never be burned into my soul
like a rainy afternoon with a guitar, a cup
of Russian tea, no television, and you
in a temporary apartment - rented in an old house
with a permanent passion – new and huge.

These words were not there for me
when I opened the diamond earrings
that you had worked harder to afford
in logic
than you had strained to afford
in dollars.

Without any words on the porch at the cabin
looking at the mountains in the haze,
I remember the prayer that brought
you to me, and Beegee, and Chad
with the plans for Dallas already
on God's table.

But these words insist they are not a poem.
And I know they are more than memories.
They are images of passion and emotions
and affection and spirit and unity.
and they are gifts from you.

Ellen, 2007

THE FLAME

Soft, shimmering sliver of flame
devilishly dancing in your hand
lighting the ceiling
yet darkening the room
and definitely opening our minds.

   Keith, graduate school

SMOG IN THE SHEETS
(A song)

Sweating away in the summer heat.
Looking at a grave yard of cars
Feels like the world has come to a halt
No one moves at all.

I can see the frustration in the eyes
While others just sing to the songs
That the local radio plays
As we inhale the smog.

(Break)
Imprisoned in my own cell of metal
The road had become my beach
Then there was you
Like a conjugal sea.

(Verse)
The road is like a jungle
So thick you can't see at all
Where are the monkeys going to play
When the trees begin to fall

You're sitting in your red car
Listening but you can hear the calls
I'm screaming out your name
But do not know who you are.

(Break)
See you in my own mind
Smog in the sheets
Then there was you
Like a conjugal sea.

(New Section)
 Where did you go
Why can't we stay
What happened on the road
I'll dream of yesterday

Some where some how
Daisies will fall
The knob is broken
Bikes, trains, and wall

Chad

THE 19TH HOLE

Busy sweeping the porch
standing crooked with one hip cocked higher
to keep the baby from sliding off,
I never imagined myself here with you
chasing a little white ball around.

No longer spending my Saturdays
with kids, clothes, and papers,
in mid-life, I've earned the right to enjoy
my week's end
and you – us.

I know that when we
leave the green on the 9th hole,
you'll pick up my wedge,
handing it to me and
with that sideways glance
and pirate smile, you'll say,
"Let's quit after 9 and go home
and fuck."
And I'll offer the expected,
"Stop that, we came to play 18."
Not once did you forget to add,
"Leave now, and I'll let you
be on top."

And we'd both smile knowing
that after the 18
we'd go home to cook steaks
and drink beer and
stare at each other
hardly believing how lucky
we'd been to survive
jobs, children, bad times
and good.
Winding up here
still needing each other.

Ellen, 2015

GATHERING
MOMENTS

THE HAWK

The sky is just preparing to burn.
The wind is quiet and still.
Up in a tree a young hawk waits
ready to do his will.

Today is the day he is going to fly.
He's been waiting oh so long.
He thinks he will fly today.
He thinks, but he is wrong.

The wind is blowing into a breeze.
It'll help him to get along.
He thinks the wind will help him.
He thinks, but he is wrong.

The breeze is blowing into a gale.
It's getting very strong.
He thinks the gale will help him.
He thinks, but he is wrong.

He spreads his wings, he lifts his legs
and perched, he blinks his eyes.
The wind propels him from the tree.
He hits the ground and dies.

Keith, written in high school

THE GIRLS

The night and day will be imprinted on my mind forever.
The first time I called friends I never called before.
The second time I was too worried to call at all.
No one understood why, and I was to blame.
But the thought of you brings tears to my heart.
Tears of joy and tears of sorrow.
I was very protective at first.
Now, I wait for that hug, the smile, and the tiny hands.
Oh how they grow so quickly.
I am asked to fix everything – from dolls, to scratches.
I would never trade this for anything.
You are my elixir of life.
You are my reason for being.
You make me mad, sad, and glad.
You make me proud and make me smile.
You can change my moods with just a simple gesture.
Memories will last forever within my soul.

> You are my girls.

Chad

A GOLFBALL IN MY HEAD

There's a golfball in my head;
The doctor wants to use a driver.
I think he's crazy.
Fifty thousand in full uniform are lighting
Zippos in my head, in the wind: they light.
All I see, feel, are the flames, the heat.
The uniforms are gone, were never there,
The applause is deafening,
The crowd aroused, the scoreboard, goalposts downed.
Some days it rains, the Zippos useless.
No uniforms appear, only the truck with the tarp.
Heliocopters fly upside-down to dry the ground,
Urge the rain home, the Zippos out once more.
Between Zippos and tarp trucks and
Heliocopters upside-down praying "rain, go home"
There's a golfball in my head
I wish he'd use a three.

Keith, 1974

NOT-QUITTERS

not-quitters
are the people
i pity most.

ones who
justbarelymissed
and even those
who were
justoutbyahair

easy if you
had never
tasted love
to go every day
in dull steps
along your unpolished path

but hard
to have it
near enough
to reach up and touch
then come back
empty

--handed.

        Keith

PULLING THE COVERS

I made my bed up today
for the first time in years;
I had not since that splintered night,
the one she spent shooting apples off my head,
with mercurial moves to the music
from the calliope of her one night carnival.
I spent that night adoring her performance—
critically acclaimed to say the least.

I folded the sheets with ease.
Perhaps I needed only to pull more delicately,
more precisely, eyes closed with concentration
or perhaps by the light
of the bedside lamp that I never use.

Dallas, 2003

TAXI DRIVER

the taxi driver
being suspicious
turned around
and blared out "hello"
as an excuse
for seeing such
a pair as us
together again
on stage
for the first time

and being thoroughly convinced
that we were
our old sane selfs
he querried "where?"
and upon being answered
"tomorrow"
started the meter
and slammed the door

Keith

PANTY RAID ON THE CONVENT

Mount your horses, men!
Tonight, we take what is ours:
those concealed women,
those servants of a silent master
who imprison themselves
behind doors of divine destiny
and expect them to open on their own.

Hold fast to your convictions, men!
And secure your cerebral faculties:
for it will take them all
to turn the virgin hearts
and lighten the weighty standards
 of those who ignore burning desire
and answer only to the burning bush.

Protect your wits, men!
Close your weary ears,
avert your exhausted eyes
to the secluded masses
for they are master salesmen of false hope
and professional at disguising
their ignorance as innocence.

Keep the faith, men!

For though the night will be long and the casualties great,

the victory will be ours—

The cloistered will finally recognize that

despite his imperfection, there is still

a great use in the unmartyred man.

Dallas, 2002

THE WALL

The night was just becoming
The horse was in its stall.
The bees had just stopped humming
When he came upon the wall.

He didn't try to scale it
Or even tunnel through
But he quit and looked for shelter
And rested with nothing to do.

But the wall it did not crumble
And he knew he had to get o'er,
So he picked himself up and struggled
To get in the race once more.

At first he had it easy
And he thought he had it right,
But he slipped, and he slid, and he stumbled
And he lost to the wall that night.

But when the sun was dawning,
He was at the wall again.
Now he was smoothly talking
Trying to be its friend.

And as a friend he went farther
Two steps farther than before,
But the wall itself trembled
And down he fell once more.

So now he was quite angry.
And now he was quite mad.
But still he lacked the wall.
And still he was quite sad.

He thought if he were better
And stronger than before,
That the wall he still might conquer
And he needed to get o'er.

So he cleansed himself of vices
And tried the good, clean way
And soon he tried the wall again
And lost to it that day.

Having tried the wall so long
He felt like giving up.
But having known the wall so long
He knew it would be tough.

He was hurt and rightly so
For he could not get o'er
And he knew that better men had come
And scaled it once before.

The wall still wants for better men
The horse has left its stall,
But he was just not good enough
To have scaled the wall.

Keith, 1977

OF WALLS AND WARFARE

"Your fragmented memory makes me trigger happy
To say things only my walls have heard."
                    Freddy Sublett

In an abandoned room,
the walls creep in on themselves,
leaving no room for the light
which exits through the cracked glass
of a single window that vanishes with it.
Only I am left,
left with the monsters in my mind
who take turns delivering blows
 to the beaten carcass of my sanity
While my muse lies bleeding in the corner
repenting indecipherable obscenities.
Confused, I scream your name against
the mighty collapse of the walls, and
with an arrogant sneer, they retreat
to their original position of imprisonment,
content in the fact that they made me
break my promise
to never speak your name again—
Another stalemate between will
and the heart.

                    Dallas, 2002

NO JACOB, YOU

No Jacob, you who lie fevered
with cool-tempered nails
and young, pale, canyoned lips.
No, you telling dreams
of old men and many steps
are not the one
of sheepskin and porridge.
You bother not with tribes
and nations---
Only a sister, frail, proud;
From her, you steal no birthright,
no blessing, just death.
Name unchanged, you lie alone,
No visions, no well—
Only a sister, deathless.

Keith, 1974

I AM THE POET
For Peter, a true poet

I am the poet, the last soothsayer,
the giver of dreams, natural womanlayer.

With loves far greater than mere mortal women.
I am the spreader of literary semen.

I am the poet, augmenter of truth,
the sharpest edge, the canine tooth.

Seeing through dimensions known not to mortals,
I travel on rainbows through imaginations portals.

This is my legacy, but make no mistake,
for I am far greater than that I create.

The symbols of ink are easily reed thin
For the power resides in the hand with the pen.

Dallas, 2002

TERMINOLOGY

Trying to teach the term "paradox"
I quote to you, my students,
Tracy Chapman who sings
    "War is peace
     No is yes
     Love is hate"
Hoping you know the song and can relate to her
    Youth and wisdom

But I never mention the irony
That you exemplify, my young friends,
That you are the personification of paradox
    You are teacher
  You are wisdom
    You are understanding
Of those questions I still ask of your
    youth and wisdom

The various you's - the paradox
    The can'ts, can
    The can's, don't
    The plain so beautiful
    The honesty in your cheating
    The hypocrisy in your honesty
    The passionate hate in your love,
    The burning love in your hate.

And for one swift moment,
I think I understand your questions,
And have the answers you have taught me.

Ellen, 1983

DALLAS COWNE'S DREAM

I woke up one day to find they had improved me.

The fences in the pasture had formed straight lines with perpendicular angles.

And they were all measured with units in the metric system.

My goat tried to eat a high-speed internet wire and was converted into WordArt.

I was told later that he was a quite popular piece.

Some suits attacked the cow.

They came in the night and

replaced her soul with a Number.

I guess she lost the will to live.

Her number was 53080302001,

I had to admit that was a damned good number.

Something happened to my dog, too.

He just stopped moving.

But if you shove AA batteries up his ass,

he will do back flips.

Lord knows what he'll do with a 9 volt.

Everything is better now.

My future is hand-held.

Dallas 2004

SETTLE DOWN LITTLE COWBOY

Tune to C harmonica.

C   F
Settle down little cowboy
C   G
Come and sit by the fire
C   **F**
No more ropen' till tomorrow
C   **G** **C**
Kick up some dust and stay a while

(Guitar part the same on each verse.)
Every cowboy has a story
Every cowboy has his time
Out on the dusty trail
Trying to ease their mind

Break
Now when you're riding all alone
With the six gun by your side
Trail will get kind of lonely
Keep a going for da ride
    break (harmonica whistle)
When tomorrow comes will be early
Under neath the deep blue skies
Settle down little cowboy
Rest your head and shut your eyes
In the morning we'll be ready

We'll saddle up and say good bye
The camp fire will have settled
We'll leave our troubles all behind

Never forget the sunset
Always remember the starry skies
Settle down little cowboy
Rest your head and shut your eyes

Chad, 1994

NO EXTRA CHARGE

death comes in all sizes
and if its after closing time
It can be delivered
right to the door.

no extra charge
for such friendly
neighborhood courtesy
but if your friend
next door or down the street
finally receives
his order
make sure you
call on him
the very next day

you wouldn't want
to miss the
show

hot dogs and
soft drinks will
be served courtesy . . .
. . . hurry hurry hurry
step right this way.

    Keith, college

SERMON 2012

Father often quizzed us
on the meaning of Sunday's sermons
redirecting my wandering mind
from personal thoughts suspended
in stained glass windows.

As I grew into adulthood,
my thoughts returned to those colorful traps
until Sermon 2012.
"Become the person God intended you to be"
said the pulpit
and I realized I had yet to meet that person.

I had acquired years of seeking answers
in a pair of Nikes
chasing the sun at twilight
until it slipped into the earth
thinking answers were at its interception
if I could just catch it.
But the road and its miles didn't offer reprieve.
Everything was never enough
and nothing was always too much.

Under guidance of Sermon 2012,
I ended the chase
and allowed myself to fall behind the earth with the sun
trading the chase of compliments for listening,
collecting possessions for simplicity,

living for accomplishments for humility,
and following bumper sticker wisdom for personal insight.

No longer chasing the sunset but falling into dusk,
there I was at the bottom
the person God intended me to meet.
And everything became enough
and nothing was ever too much.

Beegee, 2012

ROOMMATE ANXIETY

Bourbon and Loratab could be lovers—
they fit together so well
and offer your only solace
in an empty apartment so crowded
that there is not even room enough
for maturity and compromise;
You know the walls are a little too tight
when parking becomes a fighting matter
and the washing machine is a territory
waiting to be claimed all over again
each day;
Too many rented girlfriends with
rented movies collect space in your chair.
There are not enough cereal bowls to go around;
and so you go around and around
each day.
desperately waiting for someone to
fall off the merry-go-round;
one of the others
who does not contribute like you,
because you always unload the full dishwasher,
you never forget to feed the cat,
and you never leave the door open.

You would be the perfect roommate,
if only you lived alone.

Dallas, 2003

COST

How much would it cost?
to hold you for 24 hours
and let you go
and say nothing but our names
no promises or vows to be broken
no talk of love
that way no one would lie
and no one would get hurt
but for 24 hours we'd be alone in the world
I holding you
and you holding me
and at the end of a day
we would part not knowing each other
and not wanting each other
a good safe deal.
how much would it cost?

Keith, 1976

INMATE

I never asked for this,
to only see my true self
reflected
in the blade of a knife splattered red
like the quivering lips of a whore,
but my conscience affords no hookers
only garden spades and razor blades;
Liberators of the imprisoned
of those bound to veins, a life in vane
when not released by me.
For what is the purpose of blood,
If not to bleed?

I am misunderstood and do not understand
society's misuse of its great men,
to separate them from their purpose,
to confine them, like blood,
To cells.

Dallas, 2003

SALTED DAISIES

Salted daisies walk through pictures of basket weave
to find doggies that like onboard realism from afar.
These are the words that one untold dream
could find change without pain;
as though it were a manual for forward failure.
But, this pragmatism is less than genuine.
It is a meager diminution of conviction in one's accomplishments.
The blogs of prattle are an abridged amount of that
of an observation from other seedling daisies
that are fervent to experiment devoid of wisdom.
These germinate neophytes must find harmony in the existence to come.

Chad, 2013

THANK YOU

hail you, peerless ministers who have been called
to terrestrial tasks like angels fallen
on rusty beaches, poor Tybee's soil.
For countless summers, you continuously toil
to touch the lives of the young and downtrodden,
to remember those that others have forgotten;
You who count your wages in thankful embraces,
You who look for your reward on innocent faces,
You are the tongue of God to the souls of the confused,
You are the hands of God to the wounds of the abused;
For despite the hard work and occasional pain,
if you judge your achievements, you will surely find
that you are changing the world, one child at a time.

Dallas, 2005

SLIDING CHORDS CHORUS ON TOP / MAIN AND BREAK ON BOTTOM

E	D	C	D#
a9	a7	a5	a8
A	D	G	C
f5	b5	f3	b3

Skipin' and a jump'n a

Livin' it

Lovin' all around

Getting it up and

Help'N your self

up off of the ground

Getting it on and living your life

Feeling the passion Seeing the real thing

Break Yea.......A G A C A G C --- D---

Jump to the feeling ride on the grove thing

Get up and do it ain't nobody holding you back

A G A C A G C--- D---

Chorus 2

Finding the Rhythm

Feelin' it

Getting on the beat

Going with the motion

Riding it

Get on your feet

Bridge

Everybody's got some

You got to get the feeling

Why can't you set yourself free
The worries of tomorrow have only
Monetary reasons
That politics and hypocrites can't see
Why can't you set yourself free
Open your eyes and see
Why can't you set yourself free

Chorus
Skipin and a jump'n
Living it
Loving all around
Getting it up and
Helping yourself
Up off the ground

Wake up and see it living and beliving
Forget about work just kick back and relax
Break A D A G A D C--- G---
Ease your worries Leave your mind
You need no money forget all about time.
Break A D A G A D A ---
Chorus 1 2 solo section Chorus 2 1 **__End on last chord of chorus__**

Chad

GATHERING THE WRECKS

RESPONSE

Waking from the sleep of innocence in mid life,
I learn the hard lesson cutting through the silence
Of my faith like an iron sliver into my heart
--a shard of evil flickering barely long enough
To recognize the truth of it –to almost destroy faith.

Recognition of evil exploding into flames of discipline
Asking me to acknowledge it
And yet move forward with class
Accepting the gift from my enemy
--The Little Assassin—

And with a sense of sophistication so iron
And with discipline once fiery orange
Yet now ashy grey in its sorrow.
Singing the death march
Ending in sorrow's song and grief's blade
Yes—Death visited here.

> Ellen, 1995
> (On leaving our home of fourteen years, our friends, and our
> church)

53

COMFORTABLY MISPLACED

If only I'd
fed the dog
let him sleep
not married for love.

This comfort fits,
but separate visions offer no path for growth.

Tomorrow I must
feed the dog
let him sleep
leave him.

Beegee, 2010

NO BLOOD, NO GUN

He died aging, a little over twenty.
Empty-handed, she shot him twice;
There was no blood, no gun.
It didn't take long, months, maybe a year;
No one counts, really—some dinners,
a few ballgames, Christmas unnoticed.
She never forgave his neatness, the afternoon
he folded again the underwear she just folded.
Somewhere between the ballgame and Christmas
she needed to know: he told her not knowing
himself for sure. Disappointed, she fired.
He died aging, no blood, no gun, neatly.

Keith, 1975

FITZGERALD RAG

"I will live deep and suck out all the marrow of life."
                                        --Henry David Thoreau

"I will sound my barbaric yawp over the roofs of the world"
                                        --Walt Whitman

"I was so much older then, I'm younger than that now"
                                        --Bob Dylan

Rage with me brothers,
against the maturity thrust upon us
by a world we swore we'd never accept
when we made ourselves foolish with wine and women;
Help me capture the fireflies of our past foolishness
in whisky bottles and Solo cups.
Let's suck deep the cigarette smoke of our youths
as we litter on the abandoned highway
that leads to the false prosperity of someone else's dream.
Let's scatter our souls like shotgun pellets
into every STOP sign we see—
and not stop, never stop in our backwards quest
toward juvenile irresponsibility.
Let's shatter the mirror images of ourselves
we introduced to our in-laws
and strangle them with the neckties
that they wear like misguided badges of dishonor.
Let's reclaim our recklessness
in a haze of drunken buffoonery as we remember

ourselves as we once were.

We are not dead yet—
And we will not be bound to that perpetual
Monday morning grave
that others mistake for a life.

Dallas, 2003

DIVORCE

Hair pulled severely into a bun
Last effort at dignity,
She cried.
And I told her I understood.

The years of going round and round
The same old issues.
The tears- hope
The tears- hope.

Twenty three years apart,
The same doubts, the need
The abandonment, the fear.
The empty bed, for her –for me.

No Wonder Woman- I
Twirling round and round
To garner new grit to substitute
Fear of future without family

At four, pierced ears was effort at consolation.
At forty, the holes were too large to patch.
And little brothers just wondered
What it was.

The Ferris wheel goes up and around
And down and around
With holes so large to fall through.

And then the kids.

Moms secure the holes so
Kids can't fall through.
And try to explain.
Some love is empty and
That is all.

Ellen, 2015

THE RICE COLLECTOR

Outside an empty church,
She scours the ground
For the remains of someone else's joys,
The remnants of a party
That she wasn't invited to.

Dallas, 2002

UNIVERSITY BOY

The young man hunched his shoulders against the cold
His shorts no protection in the November wind.
A university boy reptilian in the weather
Walking through walls as well as streets.

His gambling with grades and girls
Threatened his gridiron scholarship.
As his ego drowned in a sea of disappointment,
He struggled to gain experience on the field.

He remembered being carried high
Like the team's trophy in high school,
And expected no difference in this place.
This place of anxiety and disappointment.
This place of freedom to fail.

But now – the girls, the games.
The pressure, the press.
No math, no English,
Just football, just enough.

And then the party and booze
And then the boys who actually played.
Then the drugs—the drunk girl
And then the rape.

Her red hair was soft
Her complexion clear
Her body limp
Her mind unconscious.

Blue lights flashed
Hand cuffs clicked
Jail cell slammed.
Life over.

Ellen, 2015

THE BALLAD OF MRS. JONES

Has anybody here seen Mrs. Jones?
Has anybody here seen her crying?
Tell her to wipe away her tears.
Her husband is no longer dying—he's dead.

Tell her to stop thinking of herself.
She better start thinking of the kid.
Ain't nobody gonna cry for her
Wouldn't make a damn if they did.

Flowers they bloom in the morning,
But they get pale in the fall.
Tell her she can close her eyes
Pretend it didn't happen at all.

Summer comes with the sunshine
And winter she comes with the snow
But rain it falls when it wants to
And nobody ever knows.

Keith 1967

NEW FOUND DISPARAGEMENT

The looking glass is broken,
and only a keen eye can see
this microscopic disparagement
that lies before the forest.
 Like a pine beetle eating away the life,
so does this inquiry for suppression
in an unprincipled analysis.
Starved of the rights that
only a deity can bestow on a man;
 yet, another call for a talent that is
disrespected with superfluous duties
and no acknowledgment.

Thrashed with daggers in the back
by the one that was once trusted
and always honored,
and giving only to be taken for the fool.
To sit so elevated in a political arena
like a supernatural being and solitary show
the uppermost level of unscrupulous demeanor.
 To think that one's biased thoughts could demise
another person's accomplishments and potential.
There will come a day, and the facts will be presented
to only find that hurting one's probability
will later cause detriment to your own for perpetuity
--in life and beyond.

Like the tree falling in the forest after the beetle
has taken every nutrient away and left it hollow,
I am hollow too. But, I will not fall.

Chad, 2009

RELUCTANT

Reluctant in an old room,
they sat among old friends
and guessed about days gone by.
Trying to speak of special nights,
they worried when this
would happen again.
They glanced at each other glaring,
hoping to see some familiar fault,
some hook to grab—
something to hold –

Some lingered through coffee and dessert,
Almost learning their old friends 'names.

    Keith

FRUSTRATION

It was a hot summer night
when the air is dry
And your hands are wet -
a night after a week of work
and the band played loud,
then slow
then for two
Not at all.

But in the light
She didn't look that good.
And she thought Whitman
Was a candy company.

Keith, 1975

FIVE

1.

a dripping faucet is unheard
it nonechoes through the hall
into the deading room where
the tv is blinking its tired eye
the lights have been turned off
and the dust is being covered
by a layer of the same
the glasses and plates
are quiet and still
the oven's cool
challenges the icebox's warmth
for the oddity of the dayweekmonthyearcenturyera
the sun comes through an opened window

2.

someone turn on the bigbrightbulb
so this dirty old blackboard
will go away
the drawings
on it
are damp with aging tears
and nothing is gained
by the harm that is done
except sominex goes up
five-eighths of a point
on the bigboard.

3.
and in the kitchen
the aging brillo pad
wasting at the sink
pans no longer
need the cleansing
their souls' are
sterling and their bottom burnt

4.
and the sun by mistake
got up today
and bragged out loud
about its strength
the little flash robots
next door
had it all wrong too
and exploded
Into the street about the same
time the cowtruck
passed by
donating a gallon
at each door
the zipcoder came
all decked in blue
and spoke nothing
of our loss at all
and when in the evening
the moon turned on
soothing over
the day's heat and sweat

I finally figured they just didn't know that you had gone away

5.
Lonely,
no desolate,
the dog
in a bright white night
on a cold bold plain
the air being snow
and the ground ice,
crying out
first royal
and then with remorse.
lonely,
no desolate.

    Keith 1977

LEADING FOR CHANGE:

Change is the latest buzz word in our media.

So much that needs this change, yet nothing truly happens.

There are those who want change but do not want to work for it.

Then there are those that like the status quo, and see no need for change.

The price of oil is up, the need for cleaner air is past due, and change has yet to come.

Farmers have sold their live stock, harvested their foods, and will begin to grow corn in place of other vegetables that we will need. There are hopes that this new oil will bring them great profits.

No one has cared to look at what it will take to harvest this corn into fuel.

The farmers will use a tractor to plant the seeds, another tractor will be used to cultivate the land, a plane will be used to dust the crops more than once, a truck or ATV will be used to observe proper growth at least once or twice a week, and then a large tractor (combine) will be use to harvest this corn.

All of this equipment will use fuel not produced by the farmer. These expenses will be passed on to the consumer, and it is still polluting the air in the same fashion. Oh what about the truck that delivers the corn to the industry that turns it into fuel. And the power needed to turn corn into fuel. Wow, that is a lot of overhead for fuel.

Now plant a tree, and pray for rain. We will need more oxygen and water from all this pollution. What if we could take water and separate the hydrogen and oxygen. That would create not only power with the hydrogen, but give the world back some oxygen. And over half of the world is made up of water that can be used.

There is your change.

More change.

A child goes through a formal education K-12, and takes many classes that they will forget and may never care to use again. This child is then expected to go to a higher education with the same principles of learning, but also learn an occupation that is not guaranteed. Much time and money is spent on this single child's education to only find that the student is doing only what they were guided to do from societal standards.

What if we found what this child's strengths were early on in life, and found what the student really enjoys in life. Then, strengthen this with a formal education structured around this particular interest and teach the other areas needed to make this form of education worth while to this student's career goals. Thus, all classes are geared according to the strengths of the student and the needs of the learner's academic needs for professional development. Would this student learn more, or continue to be bored and want to just fit in with the status quo.

Chad, 2006

THE AWAKENING:

It is time to live in the here and now.

No more hiding behind closed doors or shadows in the dark.

Such shadows can cast away the independence to converse and survive.

No, not anymore! I will not go down that easy.

I will find the loop holes and worship the life I was given to live.

I will enjoy the freedom to write and read.

The rights of life, liberty, and prosperity will not be over thrown.

The very rights my brothers were slain during the protection thereof.

I will arraign any tainted endeavor to seize these very civil liberties away.

The very people that take privileges away should enjoy their personal trial of no rights.

There are my facets in life to maintain success, this is only one.

One must be rich in the skills of many trades so that the weak cannot pilfer the right to survive.

I am not rich, or wealthy by any means in a monetary form; nonetheless, I do have the aptitude to continue without my current endeavors in life and become something of a new.

No man can take knowledge away from me.

I will continue to feed my intellect and earn my way back in the society that viciously embezzles a man's profession into a forged incarceration.

A corndog is a memory, and memories are a primary component of the psyche.

You cannot appropriate away thy wits..

    Chad, 2007

PRODIGAL SON REVISITED

He came home.
After the sergeant said, "No, Son."
And stamped the paper, **4F**
Foreshadowing a life of regret.
And Mama cried and believed he could get well.

He came home
After college days cut short.
Selling textbooks before the first class,
he set the stage for 4 F's.
And Mama cried but believed he would do better.

He came home
After the demon inside kept him from
coming home to a young wife
who believed in him.

Two children, a wife, and him – 4 souls
Broken by failure – 4 F's
Divorced and jobless
again home to Mama who
Believed his intentions good.
The fault all hers.

Jobs lost, relationships broken
And a new start in a new state
With a new young wife.
New demons, new drugs and

New broken dreams for her -
nightmares of being second
With a new baby on the way.

Another child broken by a marriage of
Child bride to childish husband.
But Mama said, "Come home.
She's too young to be a good wife."
So he came home.

Abandoned jobs, abandoned wives,
Abandoned children, he came home
Where Mama believed he would be better.
Because she loved him to death.

Wife #3 -A good cook,
Good woman
But a marriage cut short by
impromptu trips with friends,
Expensive toys and no job
Encouraged Mama to say, "Come home."

Home to stay, he tells his town
he's home to take care of Mama
who cooks the meals, cleans the house,
weeds the gardens but not the home
because she believes he'll change.

At 95, she makes the call to 911
To save herself
From his ranting, his raving,
his reliving bad trips.
Refusing to call it of abuse
She tries one more time—
believing he'll change.

Four more F's-
Three wives, one mother.
He came home.
And then the sirens, the flashing lights,
The screams, the regrets, the loss
Of a Mama who had
loved her son to death
–her death.

Ellen, 2015

GETTING ON:

The curtain closes and the crowd leaves with inspiration.
The candidate has spoken, but may not follow through.
The brick-a-bracks and the nick-nacks are at battle for which side of the shelf to own.

We find we care for something so much that the sight and sound makes us sick.
You place so much time and energy into this one thing.
Yet no one can turn away from that investment.

They will beat on the door, but will not look through the window.
It is out there, the time has come - this feeling creeps through your spine.
Waiting for the day to say goodbye, you pack your lunch and enter ahead to that place.

When I am trite and aged I will return to my long forgotten ways, and live again.
This is not a mid-age crisis, but the truth of my enter-being.
It is not a need to feel younger, but to reclaim the life I was forced to leave.

The reminiscence of a simple melody could transmit back the flashbulb memories.
The dead will reside on in our lives for ever not just through songs,
but in memories of good times and the camaraderie of genuine friends.

The diminutive creature presumes that the superior entity is experimenting with a frivolous essence that would create an inclination to reflect in false truths.

To consider this is to be an anecdote would be misguiding.

Today people can not tell the fiction from the truth, the truth from the beliefs, and the beliefs from the cultural surroundings that inhibit the lives of those that do not understand the divergence of reality and creative literature.

Then to push a cultural foundation upon others, as though it were the corner stone of all customs. To forget the historical essentials that constructed a realm of immunity to such ostrisization - then speculate why inhabitants loathe over such foundations.

You can teach a man to fish, but that will not make him a fisherman.
You can give rations to the hungry, but not compel them to eat.
You can love the descendant, but not be certain of a mutual perception.

A man will take two steps forward to take one step back; yet find he is only two steps away from the door. It keeps him here to thrive on the diminuation of the souls of time. Quitting is against the cultural belief and societal rules.

You fashion yourself a bed of ivy, and a long thread of tears.
Emotional or sarcastic behavior is not the style of the cynical popularity, but is in the depths of each soul and festers on the thoughts of the unfree.

Chad, 2015

MARCH OF THE IGNORANTS

Purple knuckles clutching picket signs reading.
    "Peace in the Middle East"
belong to the empty-headed masses whose
threats are dry from futile screams at passers-by
throwing eggs and muttering,
    "suck it you commie bastards"
each truck filled to the brim with meek arrogance:
America's diarrhea.

The uninformed form lines to shout at each other;
cussing from blood runs redder
and the true meaning of the word
Patriot.

    Dallas, 2003

THE GIANT

The giant still sleeps and the little people forget.
But after all the mud has been hurled
and the swiftboating is done,
where will be the headship in this vessel that is sinking.

When such a command has yet to look
for the legitimacy and only gazes through
the boondoggles that have been positioned before them.
The appearances and reverberations can be deceiving,
but no genuineness has been conveyed,
and the witch hunt prolongs on man's will to endure in the world.

This can only bring back memories of corn dogs at the local 5 and dime,
and a 20 dollar bill found in the market
to see a favorite motion picture that will one day be
the icon of a generation and generations to come.
Yet these memories soon turn to the scent
and sights of sour apples.

To see the air and vegetation that one has harvested
from years of justifiable duty
and to be ripped from all that was honorable.
Sour apples are merely a flavor that this person may one day tolerate.

For now the giant will sleep
and the little people will move about
making a fuss of clamor with no mentality
that the haze will one day vent

and unwrap the eyes of the giant
that even the best sawer
will never be able to hack down this beanstalk.
So will come the creation of hardships
upon the little people that will be unforgettable
until the next awakening.

Chad

TRANSMISSION FROM CAPT. WILLARD, U.S. ARMY
AUGUST 7, 1968

For every heart of darkness

there are thousands of darknesses in the heart of every man;

It takes a servant to kill a master,

a priest to slay a god—

The infant assassin does what he is told,

and the whispered voices are only obscene

to those who hear,

but the speaker is still safe

beneath his woolen sheets of logic and restraint.

No one knows, no one knows,

no one knows,

but the hand that bears the blood.

Who are you to demand the wishing?

Dallas, 2003

MADE IN THE USA

These four words at onetime were shown and written with pride.

Now you will find USA models with made,
assembled, and/or crafted in another country.

Who are these countries?

How is it that it costs less to ship parts to another country, have
then make it, ship finished products back, and still pay the
same amount after ground delivery and overseas delivery?

And the board of directors, CEOs, and other executives continue
to keep their jobs, with travel and lodge to these other countries.
Yet the product still remains the same cost, and now they want
to increase the suggested retail price due to higher fuel cost.

I say.…

Bring the jobs back to the USA.

Stop the wasteful use of fuel to ship parts to other
countries and ship end product back.

Stop the wasteful spending of executive travel, entertainment, and
lodge to other countries and give this money to the American workers.

Increase the number of green powered factories that are located
close to a distribution center for these products. Put these factories
in the place where old strip malls have failed to succeed in business.
And offer Americans jobs with benefits so they can buy a house and

not worry about health care. One benefit could be a discount on housing near their place of work to reduce the number of commuters; thereby, reduces the use of fuel and spending by these workers so they can save money for retirement or their children's education.

Chad, 2008

SUNDAY DAWN

(tensecondsuntilsunrise)
And nothing will be the same,
but it's hard to notice change
in a life measured in shotglasses
(nineseconds until sunrise)
and empty cigarette packs
scattered around a bed
that hasn't been made in months,
(eightsecondsuntilsunrise).
But eventually the sheets must
be washed 'cause the puke and
cum stains are way too visible,
(sevensecondsuntilsunrise)
and you can't pick up chicks
when your bed is that nasty
and your room smells like ass.
 (sixsecondsuntilsunrise)
And that's what it's really about -
is pickin' up women 'cause
the guy with the most wins.
(fivesecondsuntilsunrise)
and when it comes down to it,
there are no points for second,
and there's only one winner
(foursecondsuntilsunrise)
In the game of life, and
believe it: life is just a game.
Nobody cares about nobody;

(threesecondsuntilsunrise)
Everybody's just walkin' around
blind, clutchin' each other and
bringin' each other down to
(twosecondsuntilsunrise)
the shit that they're in,
and it's solid; you can't see
through it; it blinds the world:
(onesecounduntilsunrise).
So everyone is helpless, waiting
for something fantastic to come
and open their eyes to the new
(sunrise)

Dallas, 2002

ARGUMENT FOR THE WAKE

Wake up, wake up—
You, beneath the sheets:
compose your life's work now:
The possibility of apocalypse is eminent;
Tomorrow is shifting to the corner
of the plane of reality:

Listen now—
A bridge unbuilt spans no gaps,
and a song unsung will fall on deaf ears:
The sleeping make no love,
the dreaming do no dancing;
Their shoes collect dust
and exist as a blasphemy
to their true nature:

Throw off your covers—
whatever blocks you from the light of day,
and distinguish yourself
from the sleepy muses,
for the dream is merely the needle
on the compass of reality.
Each moment spent in dream
Is one stolen from reality.
Wake, work
And the two will be one.

Dallas 2002

GATHERING THE GENERATIONS

MORNING

With eyes half closed like two baby moles emerging
from the darkness and safety underground,
they stagger from a hangover of sleep
bouncing off the walls into my bedroom.
They grope, arms outstretched for Mommy,
safety and security.

I throw back uneven stripes and smooth humps
to invite baby moles into my own underground safety
and wonder if my lessons to them are as temporary
as the lines imprinted on their orange-pink cheeks.

    Ellen, 1977

STUDENT TO TEACHER

Watching you teach,
scripting your lesson to youth,
my mind retreats to the time

　　　You sat in the student's desk
　　　taking the sprinter's stance for
　　　a quick start on life.

　　　Wide-eyed, you meant to mend the world
　　　to steady society.
　　　Beautiful and bright, you starved to be
　　　thin enough to win the lover who would
　　　share your enthusiasm for life.

At 24, you have earned the expression of endurance.
Like the distance runner,
you expect to explain it over and over--
lapping the minds like miles
hoping that one time will matter.

More beautiful and much brighter you find
lover/students who suck enthusiasm from your soul
leaving you starved for energy and
thin from giving.

Still wishing I had written
literature for you to teach--
remembering the wonder in your
eyes as these words became clear to you,
watching you nudge
your students into learning and into life.

I know you are my tour-de-force.

       Written for Beegee on beginning her first year of teaching
       By her mother who thinks she is beautiful and admires her strength
       1995

FOR CHAD

Rattling the chains
of your wind-up swing
chinka, Chinka, Ching.
Beating baby boots
on the baby bed bars
whacka-da, whacka-da.
you were a music man
in the making.

Later, you escaped to mental symphonies
when classmates angered you,
teachers misunderstood you,
I failed to hear your song
of need or offer you nurture.

You packed up your mind and
travelled to a land of
black lines and dots-
sounds heard only by you-
little warriors dressed in black flags-
They saved the soul
I should have fought for.

You must have used those little black
balls falling down the lines
like bombs from a B-52-
weapons of war
on the battlefield of scholarship and books.

You have outmaneuvered the enemy, my son.
You wear the victor's medal of
practice, practice, practice
Chinka, Chinka, Ching
Whacka-da whacka-da, whack.
Jamming to the sounds of life,
sounds of making it, making it, making it.
Soul sounds of swingin', swingin' soul,
my warrior, my music man, my son.

Written for Chad beginning his senior year at VSU
by his mother who respects his work ethic and cherishes his soul.
1997

FOR DALLAS AT GHP

Exploding into the world in one tenth the time most babies use
and smelling like the one who gave you to me,
I know my life has changed with your coming.
When at ten months you cry your first poem into
my heart - "My Mama's got a bony shoulder"- you sang
and I release you to a softer shoulder to rock you to sleep.

Then you become your father's clone
serving a tennis ball, hard, into another's court
to prove your strength, to prove your power,
your control over life.
and I give you to tennis.

But now, on an early morning run
the sulfur water baptizing
the morning-hot grass
of the south Georgia where I once loved and
you began, and you are becoming,
I hear footsteps behind me,
each step, quicker than mine,
marrying concrete with more rhythm
than even the RAP you love
bursting crimson topped and scarlet hearted
past me, past the need for a soft shoulder -
exploding into the purple-green morning.
and I give you up to life.

Written for Dallas at GHP

by his mother who thinks he is larger than life and who treasures
his spirit
Summer of 1997

MUZ
A MOTHER AT WASHING TIME

Pulling the stool close to the sink
stripping the newly waxed floor of its shine
that you had so carefully put down using
your brush and your back and your time,
I studied the talents you used at the sink.

Putting in work pants later to be pulled tight
on wire stretchers used only for work pants and
to be hung out to dry, stretched tight and standing tall
as if to jeer back at their washer woman with
the promise that they would need to be redone tomorrow,
you wished I would wander outside into the sunshine
and let you do your work
 alone
perhaps dreaming of a
world without worry and so much work and
movie star lovers.

Watching you put in green liquid
to clean by hand the work pants and children's
jeans that you scrubbed hard until the water turned red,
I wondered why the green had become a red that
laughed at the washer woman who would be
scholar, poet, writer of children's books and lover.

And then I knew---my own small epiphany.
knuckles scrubbed red so we would be clean.
The red not only of blood given in love,
but of a life given up for lives,
washer woman, wound dresser, cook,
teller of children's stories and the maker
of children who would become scholars, poets,
writers of children's books and lovers.

Ellen, 1996

POP
MY DADDY AT BEDTIME

So much it took to encourage those feet
to adventure into the cold winter sheets
until he brought towels warmed by the space heater
and his love.

So much courage to touch the switch
that would take away the day
filled with white kittens and treehouses
and plunge myself into the dark
which would gobble small children
    like me
and hold us captive by the bloodgorged belly of fear
until he stole away my horrors
and bought my safety with his time
and I slept.

So much wonder and curiosity about
the black lines of grease burned by
the heat of hard work so deeply
that the Goop on the kitchen sink would
not wash away the proof of industry
yet he refused to sleep--
only resting his eyes
and his body on top of the covers.
Slipping the secret
that he would be gone with the morning
back to my mother;

yet mine in the dark.

Ellen, 1993

MY SISTER LOVED HORSES

She loved horses.
the sleek, muscular strength
and the fragile limbs that
bore their weight gracefully, she longed for.

Piles of books and charcoal sketches
piled around her small frame
in that big bed like a fortress that would
protect her from weaknesses she feared.

If she read about them-drew them – collected them
and owned them,
she also sucked the strength
from these beasts with no more guilt
than when she and I sucked the grainy sweetness
from sugar cane on hot, summer, Alabama afternoons.

Her passion was horses.
But she hungered after their strength.
and we all were her horses.
She girded saddles and un-breathed them.
She yanked the bit and de-strengthened them.
She held on to them with a vengeance
as if they were escaping her grasp.
And she rode galloping and running.
while struggling to walk.

She loved the stallions with wild eyes.
Instinct telling them they were too tough to be tamed,
they sensed the difference in her.
And she claimed them reaching far into
their beings past flared nostrils and high held heads,
into horse-souls that had once held a wildness
she wanted to claim for her own.

Hungering for someone to tame her,
she fought against the bit and saddle, stallion-like
but no horse whisperer came.
Just bottles of pills and alcohol
offering a bitter bit and
a saddle that fit her too well.

And like a trained racehorse,
wishing but unable to return to the wild,
She was off
      at the sound
           of the gunshot.

Ellen, 2007

GRANNY

The caramel colored bars striped the room
where Granny slept between the kitchen and front room
somehow symbolic of her life
torn between toil and teacups.

Squeezing a chubby arm between those bars
I reached for the silver mirror
reflecting light from the room's only window,
receiving only dim light from the naked bulb
dangling dead from the ceiling and
swaying with each adult head that
forgot to duck as it swept past
the baby's bed into Granny's kitchen.

In the kitchen throbbed the pulse of the house.
In the kitchen stood less than five feet of energy
doling out tin cups for sand pies
wisdom for reality and
apple tarts with brown crust so fragile
that crumbs begged to be licked from plates
yet so strong that it claimed a piece
of adult memory.

The hallway used for children's productions
of Little Women and magic shows
produced more Thanksgiving dinners than Oscars
and displayed the portrait the grandchildren thought
was our granddaddy but turned out to be FDR

This was the hall of unfame -- out of reach
for a small chubby arm reaching between
bars toward the noise of children's play,
theatre, and dinner table talk.
--Out of reach even after freedom from
bars and babyhood.

This first image of life out of reach
carried into a kaliedoscope world
always twisting the end of life to create
broken colored glass-pieces, beautiful
as the disorder of Granny's house
that I saw through baby bed bars - cage of youth-
creating the chaotic colored flurry of freedom,
the cage of the modern mother.

    Ellen, 1994

MAMA

The image of you with us three,
a mama with her brood (what five, six and ten?)
none of us old enough or inclined to be any help,
Is still as sharp as yesterday's Polaroid,
or today's cd-rom.
We're in a station, looking for a transfer,
or a piece of that two day old
ice box lemon meringue from behind the counter
to go with the sandwiches you brought in the sack,
on the way to Tulsa or Colorado Springs or somewhere.
Dad's not there, but you are.
Just like you were as room mother,
den mother, brownie mother, at piano lessons,
even with me at a municipal golf course at 8
in the freezing, wet morning cause I wanted to play.
Like you were typing the play I wrote in the fourth grade-even
with the blotter sheet still in.
We're on the way from five, six and ten
to being adults,
to being old enough and inclined to help.
Three knuckleheads who never doubted they were loved
and looked after, who never needed for anything,
who could have done far worse than to be with you
in a bus station looking for a transfer.

Keith A. Cowne
1995

FALLING INTO CHILDHOOD

October's son harvested a new way of living.
Keenly perceptive and habitually pensive,
he guards his thoughts
and sustains without complaint the weight of being first born.
October presented a worn world through fresh eyes.

September's son labored a rebirth of hope.
Arriving on the heels of loss,
he returned to the world the gentle spirit
of the one for whom he is named.
Often laughing in his sleep,
September taught me that genuine happiness desires no audience.

August's daughter surprised me with seasoned confidence.
Cautiously full of life,
announcing that the world will be impressed with her,
she delights in jumping in puddles
left by hard summer's rain.
August stretched the world.
We held hands and jumped into it
      Together.

Beegee, 2015

OLD DADDY

(Keith's grandfather who he called daddy
and from whom he borrowed his own grandfather sobriquet)

Belching, he put the saucer back on the table;
The cup, too, was empty, the eggs and Special K gone.
Nothing else was at the table: he went to fill his
Pockets with change and Tums. At 7:30 the day
Was already warm muggy—no need for his sweater.

Pearl was at the kitchen sink. After the eggs
And toast, she fixed his dinner, her back to his side.
He would come out to his chair, upholstered twice now,
And wait for his lunchbox, today with fresh peach
And backyard tomato. When she brought the box to him
He'd rise, say "goodbye," and walk out, closing the screen
But leaving the door ajar. She knew that. Not a kiss;
Not a hug. For forty years, she had known.

But today he stayed in his chair, barely rocking.
She had started back to the kitchen only thinking
She saw him rise, only thinking she heard his goodbye
When she knew she felt him near, knew she saw him sitting,
Knew she heard the rocking, slow, barely. What now,
She thought, what now, me with laundry to do and more to
Iron and his bus coming soon.

He turned, asking, "Would you want it
That you and I we split up what we've got, all of it, straight down the line,
you going one way, me the other?" asking now after five children of their
own, grown, and two of their
Eldest who died quickest, all grown, gone, asking
Now after five jobs, three towns, and forty years.

She laughed. She hadn't laughed the day her three boys
and a cousin brought him in, arms all packed
down tight at this side, him raving, still hot, wet
About his brother firing him, about only a little drink just this once, and
about his knife, and her boys,
Almost men, tired, the raving man before them heavy.
She hadn't laughed the Monday

he came round
After no word for three days. He fell on
The porch, puking, rolling, talking in his waste.
She carried him, bathed, him, heard him
Tell of poker and drink and ladies in Oklahoma City.
She laughed, unusual, unafraid.

He grinned at her a little, like he rocked.
Maybe he hadn't asked, but told her in his own way.
Pearl heard his "goodbye," the screen close, not the door.
She turned for the kitchen, the laundry,
And later that day, their supper.

Keith, 2003

THE GRIP OF THE OLD MAN'S PIPE

We meet at Turtleback Cabin
atop a mountain purchased by our mother
for Him
who in return built her a cabin where our family gathers.

With children tucked in bed,
we circle around the campfire -
The athlete
The musician
The intellectual
And pass the old man's pipe
sharing stories of childhood.

The beauty of the night brings memories
yesterdays trapped in the cold and distant sky overhead
and conversation buries the nights fears
of a world without him.

As
Muscles atrophy
Music fades
And words become harder to gather,
We find solace in the grip of the old man's pipe.

Beegee, 2015

IT COULD HAVE BEEN

it could have been
the morning show
down at the Sipe
obtained free for one side
of a DairyGood milk carton
shown to the thin old man
with wire rims
shaking, mumbling
at the door.

it could have been
the Saturday afternoon show
(matinee to many)
where something big and evil
from somewhere close by
meets Tarzan
and succumbs to his
irresistibly charming ways.

it could have been
except it was already dark
and the floor
(you bathed, pajamaad, barefoot)
feels too clean—
no spilt coke or M & M's.
your father, subbing
for the short plump smiling
lady (also glasses, always sweater),

hands you his version
of the world's greatest
hot-buttered popcorn—
implicit ticket for
the seat on the couch
next to mom.

Keith, 2005

YOU ALWAYS THINK OF
YOUR PILLOW

You always
Think of your
Pillow
As a ford
Station wagon
Probably cause
you can
remember them
together
that's when
you used
pillows and
stayed awake
to remember
them—
riding in the
old station wagon
all the way
to grandma's

Keith, 2003

CAMP GRANDMA

I can still remember
the unawkward mixture of childhood games
and old woman soap operas
that were my unequal substitutes
for the log cabin camps my older siblings bragged of:

We bounced from board game to card game,
from Sorry! To Crazy Eights.
If we were perfect (weren't we always?)
We were regarded with a Jell-O Pudding Pop,
The winning lottery ticket of the seven-year-old imagination;
 Just one, you'll ruin your appetite!
And I swear I have never tasted wine that was the equal
of whatever grape juice that resided
in her ancient treasure chest of a refrigerator;
 Just one cup, you'll upset your stomach!

Sometimes we'd venture into the forgotten fifties sitcom
that was her neighborhood;
and visit nameless neighbors bearing rubix cubes
in a vain attempt to quell our young adventurousness
and keep our feet on that brown deep shag carpet.
 Put on your shoes, you'll cut your foot!
Or we'd ride through the neighborhood in a shiny Caprice
with a trash bag that hung from the radio knobs.
 Put on your jacket, you'll freeze to death!
Or if we were lucky, we would go to the water park in the back yard:
A couple of kids and an old lady wielding a water hose,

inspiring laughter that a thousand Whitewaters could not match
but not for too long. . .
Put on that towel, you'll catch cold!

We always returned to Yatzee, Shirttails,
And Smurfs! The Board Game,
that is unless the world stopped turning
for whatever soap opera the almost-color T.V.
bore on its weary face.

Dallas, 2005

TOP TEN REASONS WHY MY MOM IS AWESOME

10.) You are a positive person. Negative parents usually create negative children. All my optimism, all my idealism, all my visions of making the world a better place are a result of you. I look for the good in people because you taught me to. My smile is a reflection of your own. I believe that I can change the world for the better because I've seen you do that for all of my thirty-four years on this Earth.

9.) You taught me how to love and analyze film and music. The first time I heard Iron Maiden's <u>Powerslave</u> was with you, and you taught me that it was much deeper than the bass triplets and guitars solos that everyone else heard. You showed me that "Rime of the Ancient Mariner" was great because of the Coleridge homage but that it also had a worth all its own. I search for the symbolism with cinematography because you showed me the inner conflict in the fight scene in Excalibur and explained the importance of the rain when Andy Dufresne escaped from Shawshank prison. I appreciate film and music (and have tried to teach others to do so) because of you.

8.) You always believed in me. The doctors told you that I may not make it and that you may not walk again if you gave birth to me, but you believed in me. The doctors told you that spinal meningitis may kill me as an infant, but you believed in me. Pretty much everyone told you that a 160 pound kid would get killed if you let him play offensive line on the Jackson Football team his senior year, but still you believed in me. Your unrelenting faith in me has inspired me to have that same faith in others. Every thank you I get from the kids and parents of the kids I teach is a tribute to you, Mama.

7.) You supported me unconditionally. Regardless of my particular endeavor, you showed me nothing but support. When I thought I was an athlete, you came to every game. When I thought I was a writer, you read every poem and short story. Now that I'm trying my best to be a teacher, you discuss every lesson plan, listen to every story about a student, and come to every event where anyone seeks to honor my productivity as an educator. I have no doubt that if I decided to run for office, you'd be my campaign manager. I never believed I could fail because you never let me.

6.) You taught me how to put the needs of others above my own needs and desires. One of my favorite memories in my life is when you brought Duane home, and said, "This guy needs a place to stay, so he's going to live with us until he graduates." If one of your students (or anyone, for that matter) needed something, then you would instantaneously disregard your desires, your comforts, to ensure that those needs were meet. I haven't matched your miraculous ability to give and I may never, but I swear to God, I will try to until the day I die.

5.) You taught me how to work really, really, really, REALLY hard. One of my most lucid memories of you was you grading papers…constantly - at the dinner table, in your chair before bed, at 6 am in the morning. If you weren't grading papers, you were teaching night classes, coaching cheerleading, working at the church, or attending one of the thousands of extra-curricular activities your students or your children were involved in. All I've accomplished in my life thus far, all of the hard work is a testament to the lessons in productivity you taught me throughout your life.

4.) You taught me my love of literature. Stephen King. T.S. Eliot. Walt Whitman. William Faulkner. Dr. Seuss. I didn't discover a one of these on my own. So much of my life, as an English teacher and as a human being, is intrinsically connected to my love of literature. "The man in black fled across the desert, and the gunslinger followed." "In the still point of the turning world, there the dance is." "I sound my barbaric yawp over the roofs of the world." "My mother is a fish." "Unless someone like you cares

117

a whole, awful lot, nothing is going to get better. It's not." My literary schooling didn't take place in a classroom – it happened in your lap.

3.) You taught me how to teach. I grew up in the classroom, your classroom. I saw you teach films as literature decades before it was commonplace. I saw you teach kids how to comprehend grammar, analyze literature, and write an essay when other teachers thought those students couldn't even read and write. I saw you make students believe in themselves when other teachers (and parents even) had given up on them. My proudest accomplishment in my professional career is the Teacher of the Year award I won a few days ago, but it should be hanging on your wall. Everything I am as an educator is because of you.

2.) You showed me how to be the kind of spouse I hope to be one day. You and my Old Man loved each other with the kind of passion that is impossible to put into words...so I won't try. I'm not the best husband, but I refuse to stop trying to be because I witnessed firsthand how wonderful a marriage can be when done right. The respect, the compassion, the love that you two showed each other is the most phenomenal thing I've ever witnessed.

1.) You loved me (and my brother and sister) unconditionally. Every other thing on this list is important, but when it comes to being a mom, there is nothing more important than...well...being a mom. Through all the dirty diapers, the epic messes, the sibling fights, the teenage upheavals, the college rebellions, and now the mid-life crises, you love us regardless of our imperfections. That has always been, is now, and will forever be what we need most from our Mama.

I love you, Mama.

Happy Mother's Day

Dallas, 2015

LAUNDRY ROOM LOVERS

The noise of dryers going round and round
create a chorus of laundry room sounds.
The heat and motion of clothes as they dry
begins to bring sleep to those almond eyes.

Until you see him walk in the door
and the idea of sleep isn't there anymore.
You make a decision right there and then,
that he'll be yours; - - no other men.

A date or two; that's all it took
then he found places he could steal a look.
From the conservatory, he watched you walk
with stars aligned instead of crossed.

He brought you home – the first in a while
and I knew as soon as I saw your smile
that we would be friends and it wouldn't take long
until we heard that wedding song.

I'm so glad you're my second daughter
'cause all the mountains, the sand or the water
couldn't keep you two apart
because you stole my music man's heart.

Your great, hearty laugh bettered only by his
makes me feel so lucky to have you as my friend.
but you gave me the greatest gift in the girls

for when Ellie and Madeline came into the world,
I felt something that one day you'll know too,
When someone cries "Nana", and it's meant for you.

But without them or maybe even Chad,
I'd love to think that you and I had
a special love between daughter and mother
that most girls don't have with any other
than their own real mother from the moment of birth.

But mothers-in-law, with all the laughter and mirth
can be friends with daughters-in-law on earth.
and I count myself fortunate to have you in my life
because you've made my Music Man happy
with you as his wife.

> To LeeAnna from Ellen
> Who loves her like a daughter
> And admires her determination.
> Christmas, 2006

FOR BRYAN

The wall she'd built Yesterday
To shield her heart crumbled,
lost to love.
She saw Tomorrow clearly
Your Cassandra,
Knowing all the woes of the future
Could not pry you apart.

Not a jester casting jokes into a crowd for notice,
Not a sage pontificating on subjects for esteem,
You stood silent at the edge of a group too notorious
For these antics
Listening, learning, and
Laughing at age and
What age sought to be.

Your head cocked to the right,
Characteristically dipped into shyness
When I told you I wanted
You to have my grandchildren.
And your Cassandra sent me to my room
With chocolate.

I knew that night
I needed to rearrange my heart
To make room for you.

For you were my third son,
My Cassandra's Apollo,
And the creator of my grandsons.

For Bryan who I admire and love as a son
at Christmas, 2006
Ellen

MAGALICIOUS

Magalicious to him,
I call you Constance.
Since the eighth grade,
Full faced with hair as shiny
As your braces
Planning your playground called Life.

Not a flyer, you were still
The best at a sport you chose to leave
For others that offered more challenge.

In high school, you got the name
Magalicious
And a man who believed in the magic
Of love.
You shared both interests and arguments.
And when the interests were larger
You loved.
When the arguments were larger,
You left.
Neither willing to be the one
Who was wrong;
Yet both reluctant to relinquish
The past, present, or future together.

You camped out in his heart.
And at college, he fought to
Fill your place with fearsome study
And fraternity games.
But looking around, he found you in his soul.

He saw clearly enough to realize
You were worth waiting for,
And he told Pop, and Muz
And me.

Now the puzzle pieces are in place
Creating a picture that you've spent
Your youth creating.
And I've always yearned
For my youngest daughter,
So I spent eight years
Carving a place in my heart
That would fit only you.

For Maggie, who has been in my heart for years.
Ellen
Christmas, 2006

FOR MY OLD MAN

Neglected though you were, you were always there,
unappreciated as a little league coach
and only halfway appreciated as a tennis mentor;
It is only now that I can fully take in
all you've done for me.

I remember the happiness on your face
when I took the field on Friday night,
and you were always there with advice
every time a girl smiled at me just right -
or sometimes wrong.

I borrowed your heroes;
You taught me how to play our game with respect
and lose with a smile on my face
because that's what Arthur Ashe would do;
You gave me the Tombstone Blues
and plugged me into the Dylan machine;
You taught me about that taste born of hoary nights
when lonely men struggled to keep their fires lit
and cabins warm.

You never asked for more than I could give as a son
and I never gave as much as I could,
not nearly as much you deserved;

As I start to put together pieces of my life
and get to know the man I am becoming,
I can envision the face of the man on the puzzle—
the man I will be;
I smile
because I know it is you.

Dallas, 1999

TURTLEBACK CABIN

An anniversary gift meant to be the most
romantic of the 27 years,
the top of the mountain stood empty.
On the lot below, the cabin grew on
the steaming mountain.
Named for a lane where people
from alternate worlds met,
in a series of novels read
by more than one of us,
it bore the burden of family
in both joy and sorrow.

Turtleback cabin was born bearing
two "Pack & Plays" for *isaiahandmadeline*
joining *ellieandquinn* as
four grandchildren waiting
for *londonandmora*
and baby boy Cowne
destined to be installed
as Turtleback kids.

Called "cabinet" by Ellie
it provided the hub for
bear hunts, fishing trips,
excursions into galleries
scavenging for art,
and golf games driving balls off cliffs.

To Madeline, "peaceful"; to Quinn, "cozy";
to Isaiah, "turtlefied" to Ellie "aesthetic";
to London, "awesome", and Mora, "happy."

The most important room always –
The porch, home to drink—
beer, wine, coffee
and tales, both true and exaggerated,
but always believed in the cloud of cigar smoke,
If not next morning

Its seed planted by last generation's
log cabin, built by Pop;
this one nourished by Keith
Turtleback cabin stands stalwart,
the peaceful port in family storms,
the steady ship in shifting seas of life.

Ellen, 2015

GATHERING THE WORD

GENESIS

No rib am I.
Not a piece, a part,
a portion, but a whole.
Adam and I loved.
But not a soul mate.
A rib mate,
but two separate beings
with no responsibility to our love
or a snake --only to God.

No Noah am I
warned by God to
save samples of his creations.
Not two by two,
but one by one.
One male, one female
One God.
No ribs

No Ziggurats,
no towers with babbling idiots
angering the god who scattered peoples
like Johnny Appleseed.
I hold fast to womanhood
and refuse the scattering,
camping out in the soul of God
as his factory of mankind.
--His creating machine.

No Abraham I'll be
asking another to protect me.
But is himself favored by God
and given the role of protector,
of land, of heritage, of family name,
of future peoples,
but not of wife.

Sarai I've been
with a willingness to be
used for lust,
married for pride,
and loved for little.

Thirsting for knowledge
and hunger for fruit of a tree.
Inviting a snake into my bed,
making God jealous.

So He gave me the gift.
Birth pangs!
Two gifts.
A gift in the refusing to produce,
and a gift in the bearing.
a gift worth a thank you.

Ellen, 2007

EXODUS

The Israelites, both fruitful and numerous
sons of Jacob and Joseph knew
the fear of Egyptians,
and the love of Lord.

Slave masters, forced labor
and the killing of baby boys,
Moses escaped into the rushes
and midwives looked away.

And Moses saw slavery,
and Moses saw fighting,
and Moses rescued
the wronged, the weak.
 and God said, "Go!"

Moses without the Superman cape,
Moses confused about law.
burning bushes, bare feet
and Moses hiding his face
saying, "here I am."

Water turned blood
and staff turned snake,
many miracles turned not
a hardened heart.

Frogs and flies
and a hardened heart.
Lice, cow,hail
and a hardened heart.

Locusts, and darkness
and a hardened heart.
But Moses listened
and God let his people go.
Exodus.

Ellen, 2015.

LEVITICUS

Dashing the blood away
but fanning the flames,
the priest touched the bull first
signifying a sacrifice.

Creating the odor for God-smoke on the altar,
no eating the sacrifice, Israelites made their
culture of sacrifice, a purity all their own
the first offering of Fire.

With no fire, with unknown purpose,
grain, both baked and unbaked
mixed with oil, substituted for flames
and pleased the Lord.

Sacrifice only in tabernacle,
 Elsewhere was Lawless blood shedding
so without sacrifice - no meat for meals
the offering of Well-being was Voluntary

But for Sin Offerings, mandatory
burning bulls and slaughtered sheep
sent splatters of blood to the altar
for atonement for sins unintentional.

Sins against Holy items and false oaths,
guilt offerings required money for
reparation and restitution.
Levite sacrifices, metaphor for crucifixion.

Ellen, 2015

NUMBERS

The people complained
and came the snakes.
Little faith, and an example made,
while Moses struggled to lead.

An idol, bronze snake
bold sign from God
brought the people together
for protection from serpents.

With each tribe given a job to do,
they surrounded the tabernacle.
and finally, Moses gave leadership
with Aaron counting tribes and boy babies.

And some transported the Tabernacle,
and Some carried the curtains.
and Some counted people's,
and all made restitution.

Laws from God through Moses –
no drink from grapes,
no unclean women.

Sacrifices and restitution
for Levites, for Nazirites,
for countless Israelites,
Numbers, just Numbers.

Ellen, 2015

GATHERING THE STORY

A SMILE WHILE PASSING

A homeless man was a familiar sight to each of the passersby. And there was little about this particular homeless man to take note of. He had all the typical homeless man qualities. Dirty, tattered clothes, unkempt hair, and a ratty, tangled beard. He was almost too stereotypical, almost like an extra on some bad Hollywood movie whose every layer was taken out of a prop room.

Except for the smile.

He lay there in the early morning with eyes still closed smiling. A few walkers began to notice that smile as the sun began to fill the space around him and lend an amber glow to his menagerie of worthless possessions. Did the smile spread with the sunrise? Some of the travelers of that downtown street would swear it did.

A businessman noticed it on his way to work and even slowed his gait to take in the breadth of that smile. He knew that smile. It was the smile of a man remembering better days. It was the smile of a quarterback who had thrown his last pass but had never forgotten the feel of a touchdown or the feel of a cheerleader. Also perhaps the smile of a man who played a mean guitar from time to time and could still hear the applause that followed a particularly rousing performance. It was a smile not unfamiliar to the businessman, and he began to feel it rise within himself as well.

Coming from the opposite direction was a young college girl on her way to class. She crossed paths with the business man and approached the homeless man, noticing his ragged appearance and very unragged smile. She didn't just slow her walk, she paused. An obvious, and even appreciative pause. She took in that smile and was, quite honestly, inspired by it. She wondered if she ever smiled while she was sleeping, and she quickly decided that she did not. Then she allowed herself to be amazed at the fact that this homeless man loved his life so much that he literally smiled as he slept. She was close friends with Prozac and Sertraline and many other colorful pills, and she was simultaneously moved and jealous that someone not nearly as privileged as she was could be so innately happy. If he could look on the bright side of life…couldn't she? She quickened her pace with a bit of a renewed confidence. Although she knew it wasn't justified, she reveled in it anyway.

The policeman came a few minutes later and immediately despised both the sight of the homeless man and the feeling that the sight created within him. He hated the part of his job that required him to wake sleeping vagrants on the streets he patrolled. This man was someone's father, someone's son. The chances were good that he was a veteran and had fought for this country a few years ago, and all these facts made the tedious and familiar process of waking him up and shooing him elsewhere all the more unpleasant. Nevertheless, the Captain would chew his ass if he found this smelly man still sleeping after he'd made his patrol. More likely the Captain would chew his ass once one of the college professors called the station to complain because that professor was worried about the smell of the homeless man disturbing the reputation of his precious, prestigious university. So the policeman would do his job, and that was precisely what he decided to do until he saw it. That smile. That man looked happy. He looked at peace, right with the world, and after a few moments to think it over, the policeman decided he would be damned if he would rob him of that. As a matter of fact, as the policeman about-faced and headed in the opposite direction, he thought just maybe that he'd tell the Captain to put someone else on this detail if he wanted to harass homeless veterans.

There would be hundreds, perhaps thousands of people who would pass the homeless man that early morning and into the afternoon and early evening. But it wouldn't be until another homeless man would discover him that a finger would search for a pulse or someone would finally recognize that smile, the smile of a man who has finally escaped the world that neglected him for so long.

Dallas, 2015

DADDY'S .30-.30

He took the can of Copenhagen from his pocket and packed it with great care not to make a sound. As a younger and more foolish boy, he made as much proud noise as possible while packing a can of dip, but as he settled into his teenaged years he realized that being loud with his dip can attracted the attention of parents and teachers. But on this cool misty morning, it was deer he was worried about scaring away.

He put a pinch in his lower lip, sucked on it a bit, and spat silently into a rusty, disgusting tin can. The same tin can he'd used for three years, the one his daddy left in the tree stand. The boy was here to hunt deer, true. He was here to put food on the table because his mama couldn't, true. But as much as anything, he was here to feel his daddy. When he sat in that tree stand, that tree stand that he and his daddy built together, it was almost like his daddy wasn't dead. It was almost like his daddy didn't get shipped over to fight a war that had nothing at all to do with his small Georgia town and the people in it. When he was in his daddy's tree stand spitting into his daddy's spitcup, he never thought of the morning that his father looked at him with those blue eyes that mirrored his own and told him that he had to go kill some towelheads, but promised he'd be back before the end of the season. He never thought of the fact that some towelhead got him first and he'd never see him again. Instead, he sat in that deer stand genuinely happy, because when he was alone, he was with his father. He was with his father because he was becoming his father. He had the same sorry mistake of a beard that covered only parts of his face, and he scratched at it in the same absent-minded way. He had the same ring in his right jeans pocket, because for some reason the men in his family wore their wallets on the left, and dip cans on the right. He didn't know why, and he bet his daddy didn't either, but he did it all the same. And when he could sneak away from the hawk eye of his mama, he'd only drink Miller High Life, just like his daddy. His slow progression from a boy into the mirror image of his father was natural, but it was also on purpose. Although that fact was not lost on the young man, he didn't waste time with it.

He spit again, still silent. He watched the sun beginning to touch everything on the horizon and spill out onto this land, this land that wasn't his and wasn't his father's before him, but they hunted it anyway because, by god, if nobody else was going to take the deer out of them woods, they would. He could see almost everything now, and although he was looking hard, he was listening harder. And there were noises everywhere, but they weren't the right ones. There was the quick and light scurry of squirrels and the fluttering wings belonging to god-only-knew what kinds of birds. What he was listening for was the deliberate silent sound of a deer's footsteps. Or maybe the grunt of a buck, but that was rare lately. He disregarded the wrong sounds mechanically, without having to process anything at all, and kept listening for the right sounds, The ones that could put food on the table. He leaned back a little and the folding chair groaned a bit in response. It was new and would need some breaking in. He'd almost cried when he had to replace the one his daddy left, but five-dollar Wal-Mart bag chairs don't last forever.

He spit again, still listening, still watching. Then he heard it. Not a quick squirrel-scurry, but a deliberate, heavy footfall. He whipped his head around in a motion that was as fast as it was silent, and he saw her. A stunningly beautiful doe. A perfect picture of woodland majesty and grace. He brought the rifle up in an instinctual, deadly motion and immediately found her in the crosshairs of his Bushnell scope. He pulled back the hammer of his Marlin .30-.30 and breathed deep, ready to exhale and fire when he saw something else. From behind the full-grown doe moved a fawn, not daring to move more than a foot or two from his mother's side. This shouldn't have given the young hunter pause. It shouldn't have mattered at all because a deer is a deer and meat is meat. But it did. He looked at that fawn and doe and thought about his mother the day she told him that his daddy was dead. How she cried but never lost control of herself, how she looked at him and told him without hesitation that they would make it because they still had each other, dammit, and that was something. He thought about the day she gave him the Marlin and said it was his turn to fill up the freezer. He thought about the cancer growing within her, the cancer that caused her to lose both her hair and her job at the plant. He thought about the muffled cries he heard through the thin walls of the trailer, the cries of a woman who was worried not about herself, but about the son she would leave behind. He thought about pretending not to hear those cries because he didn't want his mama to know that she'd failed in her efforts not to frighten him about the future he'd spend without her. All these thoughts entered his mind in the time it would have taken him to pull the trigger, and they caused him to pause and pull back from the scope. Perhaps they were also the cause of his next action, a thing he had never done before in a deer stand. He spit, and he made a sound.

The doe and her fawn looked up into the deer stand. Into the blue eyes of the boy. Into the blue eyes of the man he was becoming.

And then one of those eyes sought the scope again and wished a final farewell to the doe as the sound of the gunshot shattered the cool stillness of the morning. The doe took a quick step, another, then fell.

The fawn ran off immediately, no longer worried about staying close to his mother.

Dallas, 2015

144

OLD DADDY'S TURN

"It's Old Daddy's turn," Ellie shrieked, her brown eyes filling with excitement. "Come on, Quinn, let's go!"

Quinn turned slowly and didn't say a word. He nodded ever so slightly and followed his older cousin.

"Get Isaiah, and I'll get Madeline and London," Ellie bossed. "Hurry up – it's Old Daddy's turn to read."

The four older cousins sat around their grandfather, a short squatty man with thick glasses and thin hair. London, the youngest, was lying between Madeline and Ellie.

"A is for apple," the old man said. "B is for boy. The boy has a toy."
"C is for cat. The cat caught a rat."

"Uuu," Madeline cried. "That's gross."
"Ssssh," Ellie said, "It's Old Daddy's turn."

"D is for dog. The dog is not a hog."
"E is for elephant."
"F is for fish. I wish I had a fish."
"G is for guitar"

"G is for giraffe, too," said Quinn.

"Quinnnnnn," Ellie said, "its Old Daddy's turn."

Quinn looked deeply into Ellie's face and maybe shook his head just a smidgen. "There **is** a G in giraffe," he snuck in just at the end.

"H is for hotel," Old Daddy continued. "The hotel where we stayed was swell."

"I is for ice. Having ice in your tea is nice."

Madeline started to roll toward Isaiah but then reversed herself and just missed squashing London. Quinn and Ellie just looked at each other. Madeline looked at them and asked,"What?"

"J is for jail. You can get out of jail if you make bail."

"K is for kitten. The kitten's fur is as warm as a mitten."

"L is for ladder. If you break my ladder, I might get madder."

"M is for mother. You all have nice mothers."

"N is for Nana. You can ask Nana for a banana."

O is for orange. Or you can ask for an orange."

Isaiah started to leave but Madeline pushed him right back down. He was going to push back but Quinn and then Ellie both got in the way.

"We're almost done," Old Daddy said, "after I read, you can have a turn at fighting each other."

"Yeah," Ellie said as they all settled back down, "It's Old Daddy's turn now,"

"P is for poodle. The poodle's hair looked like a noodle."

"Q is for quick. Be quick with that stick."

It was then that Madeline said something that no one, not even Ellie could understand. They all looked at each other and then the old man continued.

"R is for rub. Rub-a-dub-dub, three men in a tub."

"S is for snake. There's a snake in the lake."

"T is for tree. Come out to the tree and stand with me."

"U is for underwear. If it wasn't for underwear, we'd be bare."

At that Quinn held up his hand, like he'd learned at pre-kindergarten. "Old Daddy, I've got pants and a shirt and a vest on… I still wouldn't be bare even without my underwear."

"Oh Quinn," said Ellie, "let Old Daddy finish."

"No, he's right, Ellie," said the man. "Quinn, You're right. I'll have to work on a better rhyme later. But for now, yeah let me finish up *Old Daddy's Turn.*"

"V is for vanilla wafers. We all of us love vanilla wafers."

"W is for water. We all need water to drink, to wash with, to play in."

"X is for extra. You're all extra special to me."

"Y is for yellow. Your uncle Dallas used to drink Mellow Yellow."

"Dad!" Dallas bellowed, "For the love of God. I liked Mountain Dew."

All four of the sitting-up children turned in Uncle Dallas's direction.

"Ssssh, Uncle Dallas, Madeline said. "It's Old Daddy's turn."

"Well, this is it, and then you all can go---"Z is for zoo. I saw you at the zoo."

Ellie popped up and jugged Old Daddy. "Thanks," she said, "for reading to us."

"Yeah, thanks," Madeline added, getting up and coming over.

Isaiah got up with Quinn and came over, too, like a group hug. Quinn stood over London and smiled just a whisper, then ducked his head forward and came over, too. He gave the old man some dep when Old Daddy offered his right fist to him.

"No, thank you all," Old Daddy said, happy both with his turn and now that it was over.

Keith, 2006

Dallas Cowne is a high school English teacher whose philosophy of good teaching is to support every student in both academic and extra-curricular activities. He doesn't just teach literature but coaches students in the love of the written word. When he is not coaching tennis or cross country or driving a school bus to after school activities or enjoying life with a wife and two children. He writes both poetry and short stories to use as instructional tools in his English classroom.

Charles Elder (Chad) is a music man – a high school band director and elementary school music teacher turned assistant principal. He writes songs about his wife who teaches special education, his two daughters, and about political injustice. His creativity spills over into his wood-working shop where he builds beautiful furniture, boxes, pens, etc.

Beatrice Elder (Beegee) taught English for seven years before going into school counseling. Her love for literature and poetry is surpassed only by her compassion for children – their education, their emotional well-being, and their physical well-being. Now working as Director of Child Nutrition for the Food Bank of Northeast Georgia, Beegee's pursuing a dream that no child go hungry. While taking care of her three children, she writes in her journal and composes poetry.

Ellen Cowne spent forty years in educaton as teacher, principal, and assistant superintendent. Most of these years were enjoyed being a classroom teacher of English in high schools and junior colleges. Having published poetry in <u>The English Journal,</u> and a book about the changes in education, <u>Dick and Jane Don't Live Here Anymore</u>, she loves best this small book of poetry because it reflects the family's lives and work with words.

Keith Cowne was a teacher, coach, principal, and superintendent of schools for thirty-six years. Though he coached tennis, baseball, and debate, as well as directing chorus and drama, his devotion was to literature, especially poetry. He would quickly tell anyone, however, that his best work was the three children he reared who all became writers and educators.